My Father
Myself

My Father Myself

by

Robin Cohen Reinach

Copyright © 2014 Robin Reinach

All rights reserved. No part of this publication may be reproduced or transmitted in any form or by any means, electronic or mechanical, including photocopy, recording, or any information storage and retrieval system, without permission from the publisher in writing.

Published in the United States

Central Park Publishers
New York, NY
www.centralparkpublishers.com

ISBN: *978-1-938595-02-8*

"Grief starts to become indulgent, and it doesn't serve anyone, and it's painful. But if you transform it into remembrance, then you're magnifying the person you lost and also giving something of that person to other people, so they can experience something of that person."

Patti Smith

Here's my Dad

Jerome Martin Cohen born November 19, 1928

"Ordinary father-daughter love had a charge to it that generally was both permitted and indulged. There was just something so beautiful about the big father complementing the tiny girl. Bigness and tininess together at last – yet the bigness would never hurt the tininess! It respected it. In a world in which big always crushes tiny, you wanted to cry at the beauty of big being kind of and worshipful of and being humbled by tiny."
― Meg Wolitzer,

Father Daughter Relationships—
I got lucky.

Sometimes I think I got the best of my Dad (and not the worst.) Being the *girl* had its advantages. I've been loved and petted and rescued by Dad all my life. I can't remember a time he wasn't there for me.

Dad was a major influence on my life, and that's putting it mildly!

I am so fortunate. I've known my father almost 6 decades!! That's a long time to have a parent.
(Oops, I just told you my age!)

I cannot tell you all how much I miss him already. A slow steady excruciating process of loss . . .

I'm going to tell you some things about my Dad, but.at best you'll get a taste of who he was and what our relationship means to me.

Robin Cohen Reinach
New York City, 2014

Things Dad Taught Me

1. How to handle my finances

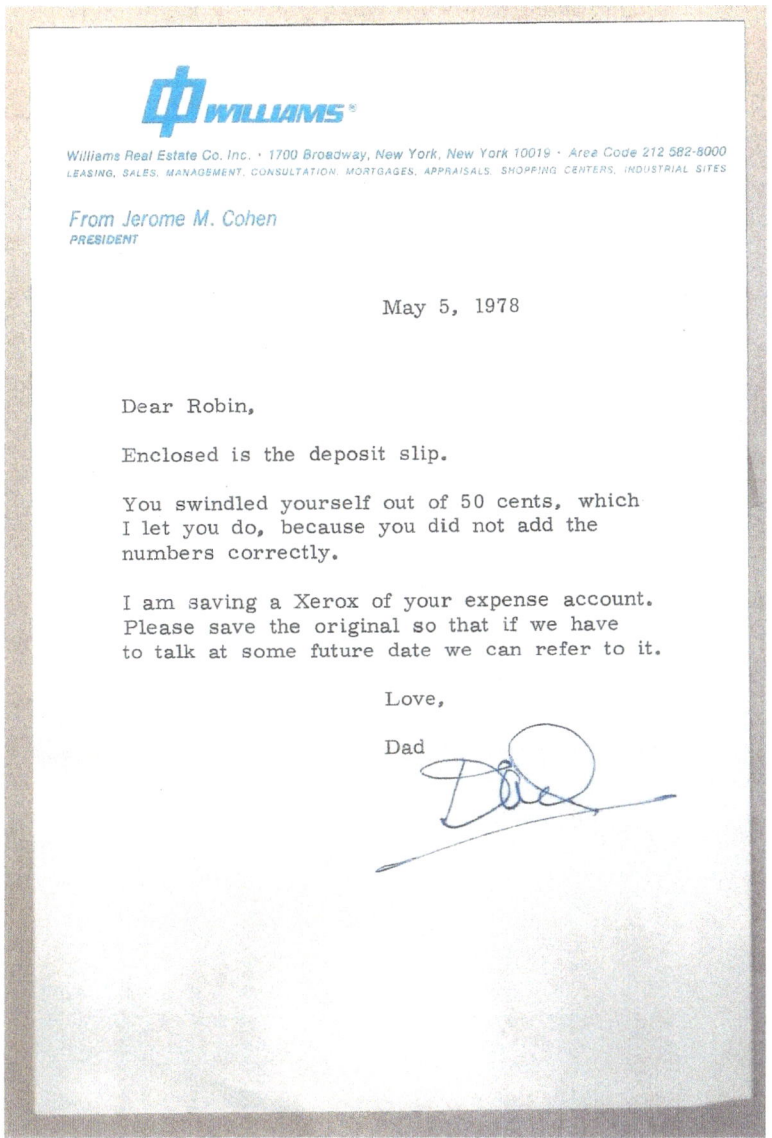

Williams Real Estate Co. Inc. • 1700 Broadway, New York, New York 10019 • Area Code 212 582-8000
LEASING, SALES, MANAGEMENT, CONSULTATION, MORTGAGES, APPRAISALS, SHOPPING CENTERS, INDUSTRIAL SITES

From Jerome M. Cohen
PRESIDENT

May 5, 1978

Dear Robin,

Enclosed is the deposit slip.

You swindled yourself out of 50 cents, which I let you do, because you did not add the numbers correctly.

I am saving a Xerox of your expense account. Please save the original so that if we have to talk at some future date we can refer to it.

Love,

Dad

2. What to expect from a man

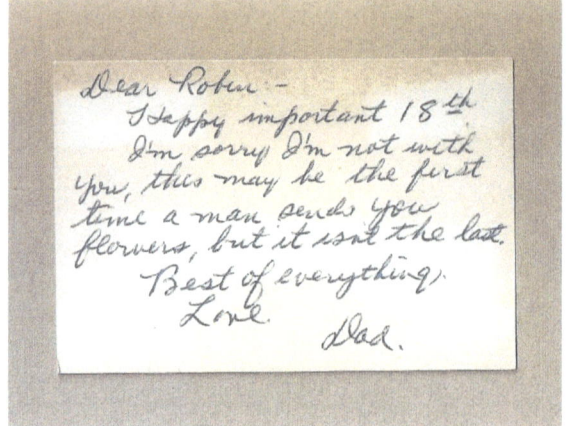

Dear Robin:—
 Happy important 18th.
I'm sorry I'm not with you, this may be the first time a man sends you flowers, but it isn't the last.
 Best of everything.
  Love.
    Dad.

3. How love can bridge a gap
                    AND
4. How to take another person's point of view

```
                    I'm Apparent


    I really don't manipulate.

    The "gap" is not so very great!

    I do my thing from love-- not hate.

    My limits on your liberty

    And middle class morality

    Are the product of predestiny.

    I groove on your maturity.

    My scene is just not LSD--



                                          by
                                 Aprowd Ad  1970
```

5. How to play 21 (including taking the seat closest to the croupier at the Blackjack table.)
6. The Principle of Supply and Demand—an early dinner table lesson.
7. How to make a bed with hospital corners (for sleep away camp.)

8. How to be a Jewish girl. Dad even gave me a manual with instructions on the topic called

What's a Jewish Girl?

by Lyn Tornabene 1966.

> *The Jewish Girl is a very special being. There are things she does and things she doesn't, things she can and things she can't, things she is and things she isn't; things she would never. . . Particularly if she's a Middle-class Jewish Girl.**
>
> **There is no other kind.*

9. How to crash a party like you own the place

10. How to feed a chipmunk named Nutsy:

11. How to cast (my favorite!), and how to bait a hook with a worm or a lure.
12. How to do multiplication and division, using flashcards snaking across the dining room table with a quarter waiting for me at the end

Dad was consistent (in an inconsistent sort of way.)
And he loved to show off!
Dad stayed in shape without working out.

Dad wasn't afraid to make a bold statement.

Dad always had his own sense of fashion.

Games Dad Played

1. **Backgammon**: My best chance lay in letting my luckiest friend roll the dice while I moved the pieces.

2. **Chemin de Fer**—How Dad loved to call out "Banco!"

3. **Blackjack**

4. **Crap**: Dad once brought home a green felt crap board from Las Vegas. He laid it out on the living room floor while entertaining. From inside my bedroom late at night, I recall hearing Dad call out "Four the hard way!" or "Goose eggs!"

5. **Monopoly**: Family real estate games were mandatory. I know all the rents by heart.

6. **Milles Bournes**: To encourage our French, Dad played this card game about driving with Michael and me. But I found all the cards with names like *pneu à plat* confusing. I didn't know much about driving either.

7. **Poker**: Sunday night, penny-ante poker, where Dad won back my entire weekly allowance.

8. **Ping pong**: Dad taught Michael and me when we went to a resort and it rained. (It always rained.)

Dad rocked the **Ping Pong Team** at Columbia Grammar

9. **Pinball:** Pinball Wizard-Dad taught Michael and me how to manipulate those flippers when we went on family vacation 1960's.

10. **Checkers**

11. **Chinese checkers**

12. **Magic tricks**: One year Dad performed for my birthday party, amazing my entire class

**Michael became a magician too. He still attends magician conventions with his kids.

13. **Bridge**

Wednesday, October 22, 1969 Dad's Bridge Game made *The New York Times*

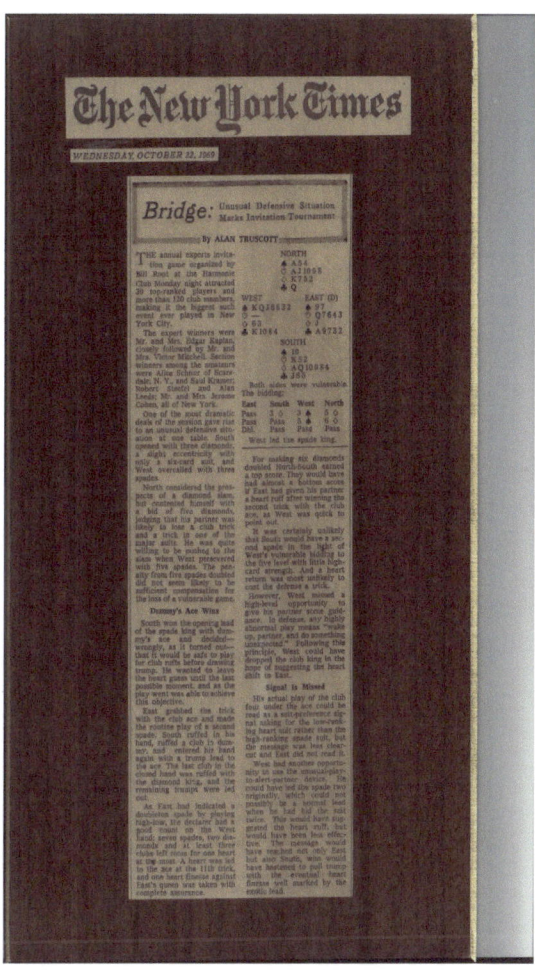

14. Agile and quick, Dad was on the **Swim Team**.

15. Always thinking a few moves ahead, Dad played on the **Chess Team**.

Cannes, France 1978

Dad's Strange Eating Habits:

1. Meat/ fish/ fowl on one plate, green vegetable and starch each served in separate glass bowls so no food contaminated another. Dad ate the protein first and then rotated each side dish into play. Dad did not eat stews.[1]

2. Snacks: Drinking Rice Krispies from a tall glass (!), and eating hunks of iceberg lettuce while watching TV

3. Breakfast—weekdays: 4 *coddled* egg yolks; Orange juice, fresh squeezed, strained for pulp and seeds. *"Start the electric juicer when you hear my footsteps come out of the bedroom."* (Fresh is fresh, after all!) On weekends: add an entire rasher of bacon, cooked till chewy, NOT crispy.

---

[1] Except Bouillabaisse in France

4. Paper (lined or unlined)[2]
5. No spices or herbs of any kind. Only salt, pepper and garlic.
6. Bread was never served with dinner in our home. We had an unusual variety of potatoes and rice, with very little pasta. I later realized this was because of Dad's Celiac Sprue.
7. Dad drank a gallon of Lipton tea with tons of sugar every day.

When I was growing up,
Dad smoked 4 packs of Kents a day!

---

[2] I have witnesses!

Things Dad Told Me

1. Don't teach your grandmother how to milk ducks.

2. Don't count your hatches before they chicken.

3. Never open a restaurant. (Too much inventory spoilage)

4. When choosing an apartment, insist upon extra closets and bathrooms.

5. Some women would rather not know.

6. Couple relationships are like swimming; someone swims beside you for a while and then you swim off on your own again.

7. If you want to understand someone's motivation, look at the result of their actions.

Here is the beginning of an epic poem Dad read to Michael and me so often that I memorized it.

Plot spoiler: The poem describes the survival of a marooned sailor who stayed alive through cannibalism!!!

The Yarn of the Nancy Bell

'Twas on the shores that round our coast
From Deal to Ramsgate span,
That I found alone on a piece of stone
An elderly naval man.

His hair was weedy, his beard was long,
And weedy and long was he,
And I heard this wight on the shore recite,
In a singular minor key:

"Oh, I am a cook and a captain bold,
And the mate of the Nancy brig,
And a bo'sun tight, and a midshipmite,
And the crew of the captain's gig."

W.S. Gilbert

What do you suppose Dad had in mind as the moral of this story? He used to chuckle when reading the refrain aloud.

The Boat

Dad loved the boat.

                        I hated the boat.
                     (I was a teenager.)

Dad's astrological sign: **Scorpio**

Scorpio Characteristics:

Symbol: The Scorpion
Element: Water
Group: Intellectual
Polarity: Negative
Favorable Colors: Dark Reds, black
Chinese Counterpart: Pig

Ruling Planet: Pluto, Mars
Cross/Quality: Fixed
House Ruled: Eight
Opposite Sign: Taurus
Lucky Gem: Opal
Period: Oct 23 - Nov 21

Uh-oh!! I'm Taurus, the "Opposite Sign"

For many years, Dad wore a 14 K gold scorpion on a chain around his neck.

Matches from the boat

Things Dad Gave Me

1. My first bouquet of roses

2. An annotated copy of *Everything You Always Wanted To Know About Sex But Were Afraid to Ask* with Dad's own comments in red Flair, his emphatic capital letters, his exclamation marks in the margins.

3. Suede fringe jacket for my 15th birthday. Mom called it "Daniel Boone with spaghetti."

4. Permission to go to Bethesda Fountain in Central Park when other kids were forbidden.

5. An index card to carry in my wallet with lawyers' home and office phone numbers in case of arrest.

6. A card game called *Coup D'etat.*

7. Diamond stud earrings

8. The first Apple personal computer

9. A 250 person Kosher wedding at the Pierre Hotel, February 9, 1986.

Flashback to Before My Time

Poppa Victor, Dad and Granny Rae

1938 Dad with best friend
Cousin Irma Oelbaum

1946

1948 Irma Oelbaum Davidson's Wedding

Hi Robin.

It's always so good to see Robin on my mail list. You seem to constantly have a project in work and I hasten to answer while I am still able.

Starting in the bottom row—That's Doris Rich on Dad's right with Stanley (Buddy) Rich on her right. On Dad's left is Irma Oelbaum Davidson, this was at her wedding, and then her husband Charles, a nice guy. She was only 18 and couldn't wait to get away from her father, Uncle Henry, and Mother, Aunt Sally. Then the youngest, Phyllis Oelbaum, Uncle Jerry's youngest. She's in a senior residence on Long Island. Brother takes care of her finances, etc. She never married. First on the next line is Marcia Rich, then my Sister Sylvia who was pregnant with Carol, then me, pregnant with John and husband Bud and Millicent Oelbaum Best, Irma's younger sister.

Next row, it took me a while, but it is David Oelbaum, Uncle Jerry's son and Phyllis older brother. Then Milton Landis and Granny Rose. Back row, Richard Brun and Marcia Oelbaum Brun, Alvin Oelbaum with his first fiancée who was a grand-daughter of Pinky Cohen, then Claire and Brother Dinhofer.

This is one of my favorite photos. John is 66 years old this month and so that dates the picture. What a load of stories relates to each of us. This was a very close family, before TV and cell phones. There was always a reason to get together and have fun. I believe the wedding was at the Alden Hotel which was on Central Park West.

Love and Kisses, Marcia

PS These were all of Grandma Rose's grand-children. We were all very close cousins because the parents were close. Uncle Abe and Aunt Helen Faust Oelbaum (First cousins on their Mothers side) Estelle Oelbaum Dinhofer Cohen, Jerry Oelbaum, Helen Oelbaum Rich, Henry Oelbaum, Rae Oelbaum Cohen, in order of birth. One every year—boy girl boy girl boy girl.

Titanic Pose 1954

Mom and Dad look incredible for a hot second! Could there have once been that much passion?

It was a Strange and Deep Marriage from the start.

May 20, 1956
In the hospital on the day I was born: Dad, Granny Rae, Mom

I love Granny and Poppa
1970—God Bless

Cohen Family 1972 with the Berlin Bear

1982

My Family of Origin

1977

1989

Symbols.

To one of Chinese descent, this means Mother China.

To all real estate men, this means Square Feet.

To metropolitan New York, this means Williams.
It is our new symbol, more seen and more recognized every day—our new *forward* look.

Williams & Co. Inc. · Real Estate · 1700 Broadway, New York, New York 10019 · Area Code 212 582-8000
LEASING, SALES, MANAGEMENT, CONSULTATION, MORTGAGES, APPRAISALS, SHOPPING CENTERS, INDUSTRIAL SITES

Dad placed this ad in the Lenox yearbook, and I thought it was so clever.

1980 Dad's terrace at the Sovereign

These photos were taken for a brochure I wrote for Williams while in grad school

Dad with Poppa Victor and Ed Roos 1955, the year before I was born

1986 Father and Son in Real Estate

Tuesday, September 4, 1951

Fathers and Sons in Real Estate

Jerome M. Cohen and Victor J. Cohen of Williams & Company, Inc. specialists in management and sales of loft and commercial buildings in the midtown area. Mr. Williams, president of the firm, founded it about 25 years ago. Jerry joined his father a year ago after graduating from Syracuse University where he majored in English (wrote his thesis on real estate, he hastily adds). Recent outstanding deals of Williams & Company include the sales of the Lefcourt Central Building on W. 47 Street and 70 West 40 Street. The firm also manages these buildings.

Buildings Dad Talked About

1. **D & D Decoration and Design** building—an Industry gathered in a single office building, Dad's idea!

2. **1700 Broadway**—A risk, too far uptown on West 54th Street for an office building

3. **9 West 57th Street**—multi-year law suit over largest real estate commission ever paid at that time. After many years, Dad won!

4. **1 Dag Hammarskjold Plaza**—Another risk, but near the UN. Dad showed my boyfriend around the building during construction. They both wore yellow helmets.

5. **28 west 23rd Street**— Renovation, restoration, the atrium like the famous Plaza Athena hotel in Paris (where the Cohen family stayed in 1972),Dad received the Distinguished Citizen Award

granted by the 23rd Street Association for giving new life to the entire neighborhood, where a great renaissance occurred.

6. **655 Madison Avenue**—First prestigious uptown storefront with Madison Avenue quality boutiques.

7. **57 west 57th Street**

Dancing with Dad at my wedding. Feb 9, 1986

Grandpa

A tender and proud gaze at the only male in the next generation, grandfather to grandson.

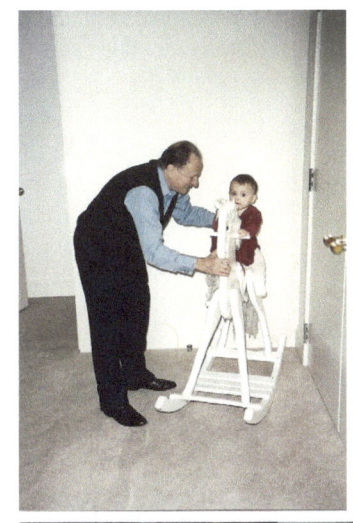

Dad was gentle with Jess

1995

1997

When I planned this family spring vacation to Florida, it made Dad so happy that he declared I had given him the best gift a daughter could ever give.

Dad was featured in *The Calhoun Chronicle* in an article about grandparents who were taking a special interest in their grandchildren. 2003

2006

The Long Good-bye

Dad, you were so brilliant
we didn't notice at first
that you were fading.

November 19, 2006

Ever the Proud Patriarch

Jerome Cohen's
83rd Birthday
November 19, 2011

Robin and Michael Cohen invite you to celebrate and honor our Dad among family and a few close friends at the home of:

Robin Cohen Reinach
115 Central Park West
#15 C
Saturday,
November 19
at 6 PM

RSVP to
robinreinach@gmail.com   or 212-874-7236

Please join us for an informal evening. A buffet dinner will be served.

On Dad's 83rd birthday,
I gathered the family at my house.
Milton Dinhoffer even flew in from California.
We all knew we were saying good-bye.

Dad's 83rd Birthday
November 19, 2012

Standing: Gleniss Schonholz, Lyris Schonholz, Jay Dinhoffer, girlfriend, me, Michael T. Cohen, Mom, Irma Oelbaum Daivdson, John Teschner,
Sofa: Marcia Teschner, Elizabeth Cohen, Dad, Jessica Mastro, Susan Mellis, Natalie Cohen
Floor: Zachary Cohen, Juliette Cohen

Dad gets a
Lifetime Achievement Award
at the office.

Realizing it's the LAST time my family of origin will EVER be together (*alive*), I hand off my iPhone, and get this final picture—2012

Dad and I take a Double Selfie
2013

Dear Dad,

The voice in my head sounds like you.

Love, Robin

The words that a father speaks to his children in the privacy of home are not heard by the world, but, as in whispering-galleries, they are clearly heard at the end and by posterity.

~Jean Paul Richter

There's something like a line of gold thread running through a man's words when he talks to his daughter, and gradually over the years it gets to be long enough for you to pick up in your hands and weave into a cloth that feels like love itself.

~John Gregory Brown

Dad's 85th Birthday. November 19, 2013

Dad,
Michael and I are both part of you:
yin and yang.
Going forth into the world
with love and integrity,
we honor you.
Your essence lives on.
Love is forever.

Robin Cohen Reinach
August 2014, New York City

www.ingramcontent.com/pod-product-compliance
Lightning Source LLC
Chambersburg PA
CBHW041220070526
44584CB00001B/24